The Life of Paul Revere

Molly Mack

INFOMAX COMMON CORE READERS

Rosen
Classroom™

New York

Published in 2013 by The Rosen Publishing Group, Inc.
29 East 21st Street, New York, NY 10010

Book Design: Michael Harmon

ISBN: 978-1-4488-9049-1
6-pack ISBN: 978-1-4488-9050-7

Manufactured in the United States of America

CPSIA Compliance Information: Batch #WS12RC: For further information contact Rosen Publishing, New York, New York at 1-800-237-9932.

Word Count: 458

Contents

Who Was Paul Revere?

Have you ever heard of Paul Revere? He was an important American. He lived a long time ago.

Paul was born in 1734. He came from a big family.

He had a lot of brothers and sisters. Paul was the oldest boy.

Paul lived in Boston with his family. Boston was one of America's first cities. You can still visit his house today!

Silversmiths

Paul went to school until he was 13 years old. He left school so he could work for his dad. His dad was a silversmith. Silversmiths make things out of silver.

Paul's dad owned a shop. He taught Paul how to be a good silversmith. Paul liked working with his dad. They made things like spoons and plates.

When Paul was 19, his dad died. Paul was too young to work in the shop by himself, so he signed up for the army. He stayed in the army for 2 years.

After the army, Paul became a silversmith again. He was a silversmith for the rest of his life. Sometimes, he made things out of gold or other **metals.**

What Did Paul Make?

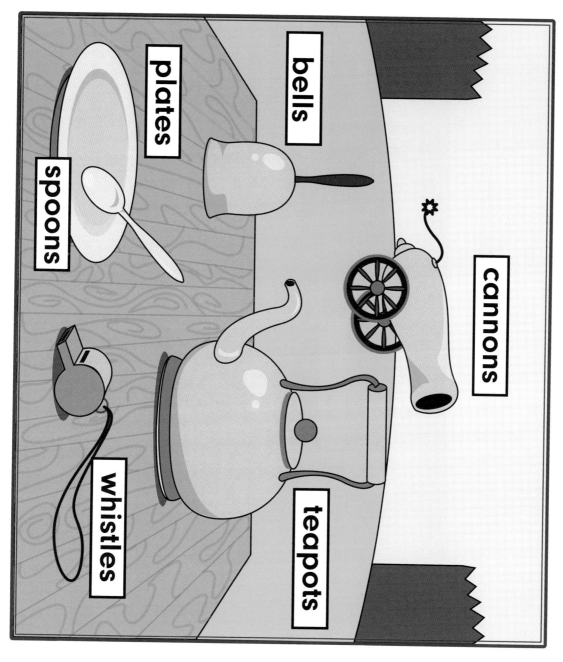

The American Colonies

America used to be a group of 13 colonies. A colony is land that belongs to another country. The colonies belonged to England when Paul was alive.

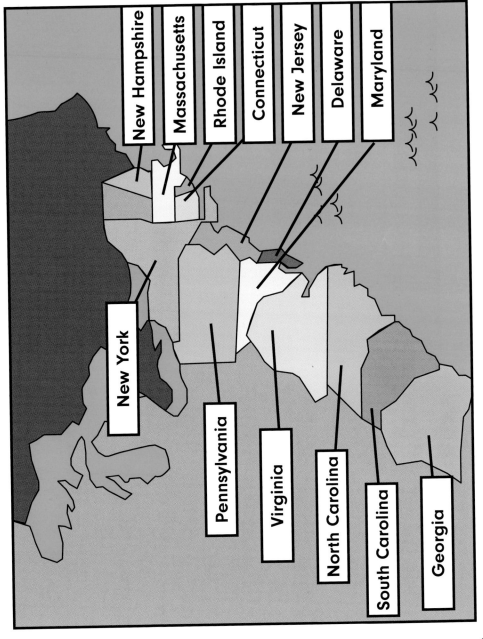

Many Americans wanted to be free. Being free means that no one can tell you how to live. The colonies wanted to fight England so they could be free.

In April 1775, Paul learned that English **soldiers** were coming to his town to stop what the Americans were doing. The soldiers wanted it to be a surprise.

Paul knew he could help his town. He decided to tell all his neighbors that the soldiers were coming.

Paul rode his horse from town to town. He rode very fast so he could tell everyone. He wanted to keep everyone safe.

Paul did this when it was very late. It was almost **midnight**! It was very dark outside. People call this his "Midnight Ride."

Paul knew that the ride might get him in trouble, but he did it anyway. He wanted to help America be free.

This made him a hero.

This was one of the first **events** in America's war to be free. People thought Paul was very brave for helping his town. The war ended a few years later, in 1783.

We Remember Paul

Paul died in 1818 when he was 83. He did many important things for his town, but people remember him for being a hero.

One way we remember Paul is through a **poem**.

In 1860, Henry Wadsworth Longfellow wrote a poem about Paul's Midnight Ride.

People all over America read the poem and learned what Paul had done. They were proud of him. Paul was a great American.

Glossary

event (ih-VEHNT) Something important that happens.

metal (MEH-tuhl) Hard matter that is shiny.

midnight (MIHD-nyt) The middle of the night.

poem (POH-uhm) A kind of writing that has words that rhyme.

soldier (SOHL-juhr) A person who fights in the army.

Index